# Gold as Your 3rd Child

# Gold as Your 3rd Child

**Manish Garg**

Worldwide Published by

Pendown Press

**PENDOWN PRESS LLP**
**An ISO 9001 & ISO 14001 Certified Co.,**
**Regd. Office:** 3767A, Kanhaiya Nagar,
Tri Nagar, Delhi-110035
**Ph.:** 8130886000, 9650072927, 8595249536
**E-mail:** info@pendownpress.com
**Branch Office:** 1A/2A, 20, Hari Sadan, Ansari Road,
Daryaganj, New Delhi-110002
**Ph.:** 011-45794768
**Website:** PendownPress.com

**Edition:** 2024

**ISBN:** 978-93-5554-756-9



*Layout and Cover Designed by* Pendown Graphics Team
*Printed and Bound in India by* Thomson Press India Ltd.

# TABLE OF CONTENTS

# Preface

Have you ever dreamt of a financial future overflowing with stability and security, not just for yourself, but for your loved ones as well? Perhaps the world of investments seems daunting, filled with jargon and complex calculations. If so, welcome, for within these pages lies a journey that transcends the traditional and unlocks the potential of gold as a cherished member of your financial family.

Witnessing the enduring legacy of gold firsthand, I embarked on a quest to demystify its role as a powerful financial tool. This book, "Gold as Your 3rd Child," isn't simply a collection of investment strategies; it's a testament to the transformative power of including gold in your financial journey.

Here, you won't find cold, impersonal advice. Instead, I compare gold to a "3rd child," a metaphor that underscores the care and planning it deserves. Just as you wouldn't neglect your children's well-being, this book guides you on nurturing gold's potential to secure your financial future for generations to come.

Whether you're a seasoned investor or just starting out, feeling overwhelmed by financial complexities is completely understandable. This book is your compass, explaining the intricacies of gold investments in clear, accessible language. We'll navigate the delicate dance between emotions and financial decisions.

Together, we'll uncover the timeless wisdom that gold imparts, transforming it from a glittering metal into a guiding light of financial security for you & your loved ones. So, step into this journey with me, and let's discover the secrets to weaving gold's brilliance into the fabric of your financial legacy.

It's a way to build a strong financial future, one golden step at a time...!

**Manish Garg**

# Acknowledgements

I want to extend a heartfelt thanks to all the people who contributed to making "Gold as your 3rd Child" a dream come true. Your support and belief in me have been amazing.

First and foremost, I would like to express my gratitude to my parents, Mr. Naresh Kumar Aggarwal, and Mrs. Maya Devi Garg, as well as my grandparents. They have not only been sources of inspiration but also lifelong teachers, instilling moral values in me. From childhood, I have seen and learned the importance of living a fulfilling life by serving the community around me. Your love and encouragement made me who I am today.

I am thankful to my beloved Guru's Akshar bhai, Swami Eshaan Mahesh & my mentors Abhinav bhai, Pawan bhai, Amit bhai who opened up a realm of opportunities across various aspects of my life by giving an eye-opening mantras and sutras of life, guided me towards achieving both inner and outer success. Their teachings truly transformed my way of thinking, and I owe the creation of this book entirely to them.

My appreciation goes to my dedicated wife, Suchi, for her continuous care and support at home. Her dedication in managing household responsibilities and the upbringing of our children has allowed me to focus on writing, and I couldn't have done it without her. You've been there for me throughout this writing journey, and your belief in me is what this book is built on.

To my team at Aggarwal Abhushan Group, you've worked really hard, and our success is because of your dedication. Each one of you has been a pillar of my success, and I'm always proud to have such a great team. My Customers, you've trusted us and stayed with us, helping our business move forward. Your feedback and support mean a lot to us. Friends and Well-Wishers, who cheered me on, thank you for believing in what I do. Your positivity kept me going. My friends have also been a great source of encouragement.

Lastly, I want to thank God for giving me the energy and clarity to write this book.


Lots of Love,

**Manish Garg**
**May 18, 2024**

# 1

# Introduction - Jaan - Pehchaan: "Mujhse aur Mere 3rd Child se"

## *Why this Book?*

In the glistening world of jewels and financial foresight, I, Manish Garg, welcome you to a journey that takes you beyond the scope of traditional investments. As an Information Technology Engineer from ITM Gurgaon and MBA in International Business from Delhi School of Economics, Delhi University, a born Gemologist & a certified Diamond Grader from GIA America, my journey into the reality of retail jewelry over the past 15 years has been nothing short of transformative. Being the eldest son of my family, I barely allowed my family's resplendent legacy and laurels to sit lightly on my shoulders. Born with a silver spoon, wisdom, and legacy from my father, I wanted to convert a wonderfully nurtured jewelry outlet into a highly professional and leading jewelry brand in the industry. And today, at the age of 40, I've realized that **"business can never be successful if it's not useful for your people, their people & their families further."**

Surrounded by the sparkle of gemstones and precious metals, I found myself drawn to the enduring legacy of **Gold - an ageless symbol of wealth and stability.** This fascination, mixed with a strong belief in the transformative power of smart financial decisions, **inspired me to pen down the pages of "Gold as Your 3rd Child."**

## Concept Decoded: Why 3rd Child?

In a world characterized by economic fluctuations and uncertainties that threaten financial well-being of individuals, as someone who has witnessed the ever-changing tides of the jewelry business, I have witnessed firsthand the crucial role gold plays in securing financial legacies across generations.

This book isn't just a list of investment tips; it's a testament to how gold can shape your financial path. Why write about gold? Because, in my view, gold is not just an asset; it is a family member, a guardian of prosperity that, **much like a third child, demands attention, care, love, and strategic planning.**

Comparing gold to a "3rd child" might seem unusual, but it captures the essence of my message, **my love for Gold as I love my 2 children.** Somebody who has only one child, can definitely consider Gold as his/her 2nd child and so on, to walk with me through the journey of this book. This book delves into the nurturing and lasting qualities of gold, which can offer financial security not just for us, but for our future generations too.

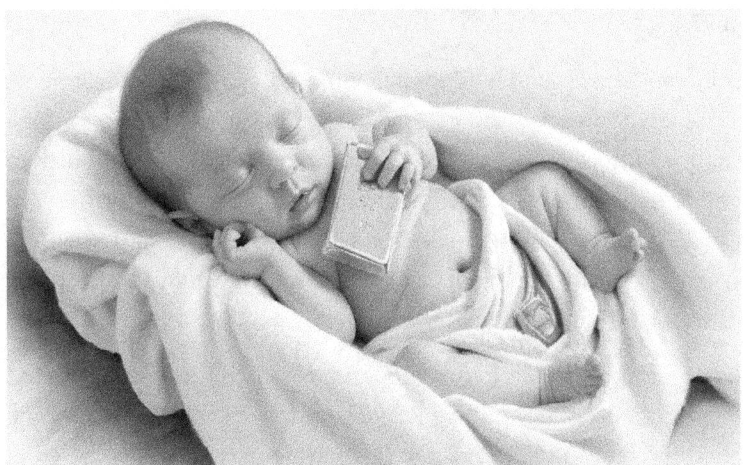

### *Sharing My Journey:*
### *Education se Business se back to Education*

Always on my toes, always excited to learn, kab mein education se business se fir se education pe aa gaya, pata hi nahi chala. This book is not just a documentation of my personal journey; but it's a deliberate effort to transfer the valuable knowledge and experience to those who seek financial empowerment. My ability to learn from others both in college life & in real life has equipped me with insights that I am eager to share with the millions here.

## *Who is This Book For: The Right Audience*

This book is tailored for individuals like me—those who find themselves little less comfortable with the complexities of finance and accounting, and might feel lost when it comes to figuring out when, where, and how much to invest their hard-earned money, their life-long savings. **If the reality of investments seems difficult, or financial terms feel like a foreign language, this book is your guide.**

Join me as we understand the intricacies of gold investments together, addressing the questions of those eager to secure their financial future with confidence and manage the tricky **balance between emotions and financial decisions.** "Gold as Your 3rd Child" is not just a guide; it is an invitation to rethink how you invest, to consider gold not just **as a commodity but as a cherished member of your financial family.**

As we embark on this journey together, let us discover the timeless wisdom that gold imparts and uncover the secrets to weaving its brilliance into the fabric of our financial legacy.

> Welcome to a world where gold isn't just an investment - it's a family.
>
> **- Manish -**

# 2

# Gold is than Most Important family member" - papa hamesha kehte hain!

## *The Man Behind the Inspiration*

There are certain voices that echo louder than others in our lives, and for me, one such guiding voice has been that of my father.

My father, **Mr. Naresh Kumar Aggarwal,** is an epitome of resilience and foresightedness. He's not just my dad but also my mentor, always reminding me of the importance of good judgement, hard work, and a forward-thinking mindset. Raised in modest surroundings, he strongly believed in the transformative power of both education and hard work to change one's life. His unwavering commitment to these principles propelled him from humble beginnings to a position of influence. From the careful attention he paid to financial planning to the emphasis on the long-term perspective, his teachings have become the cornerstone of my approach to **business as well as investment.**

## *A Salute to My Father - The Guiding Light*

In the daily bhaag-daud of life, we often find ourselves guided by the wisdom handed down from those who walked the path before us. In my case, the source of that guiding light illuminating my path is none other than my father, a man whose values and insights have profoundly shaped my journey - personally, professionally and socially.

This chapter and this book are not just an acknowledgement to my father; they are an exploration of the profound impact that a parent's principles can have on shaping one's financial philosophy. Through the lens of his teachings, we will unravel the timeless value of gold and its role as a guardian of familial prosperity.

## A Golden Lesson

One lesson stands out—a lesson that forms the crux of 'Gold as your 3rd Child'. Dad believed in owning tangible assets like gold to stay secure in uncertain times. The concept of gold as a third child was not just a metaphor; it was a practical strategy he implemented to ensure stability and security for our family. Not only did he apply it, but he also made sure that we, all three brothers, learned the same for our family and future generations too.

## The Legacy Continues

As I began my journey in the retail jewelry industry, his wisdom became my guiding force, helping me navigate the complexities of the business. His love for gems and precious metals, especially gold, fueled my own fascination, propelling me to delve deeper into the world of gemology and diamond grading. This prompted me to transition my career from a technology company to **a legacy business focused on "turning dreams into reality through Gold"**.

Join me in this chapter as **we pay gratitude to my father, whose legacy extends beyond our familial ties**—an inspiration that transcends generations and forms the foundation of the financial wisdom shared within these pages.

# 3

# Know Your Gold to Grow Your Gold! - "Kyunki Janna Zaroori Hai!"

## *Historical Significance of Gold*

As we step into the world of investments, let me share stories that resonate through the ages - stories of gold. More than just a metal, it has been **a timeless buddy in the journey of wealth, loved for its beauty and valued for its stability.** Throughout history, India has been symbolized as "Sone ki Chidiya" (the Golden Bird), inviting readers to understand the multi-faceted nature of gold as an investment. In this chapter, we'll look at the personal and historical sides of gold as an investment, drawing inspiration from tales as old as time.

Imagine ancient times, with markets filled with shiny gold and people swapping/exchanging gold coins as currency. This is not just history; it's proof of how gold has been important for a really long time. The stories about gold passed down through generations show that **gold is more than just an investment - it's a storyteller of our shared history.**

## Why Gold?

**First things first - why do people love gold so much?** Well, let's chat about it. Gold has some cool qualities that make it hot. It's kinda rare, high in demand, valued as currency by the whole world, doesn't wear out easily, and looks pretty nice when worn as jewelry. This book will talk about these timeless features in detail that make gold a big deal in our day-to-day life.

## Gold as a Store of Value

Now, here's the juicy part — **why gold is so valuable.** Remember the stories your grandparents told? How a small piece of gold or a gold coin, kept safe, became a symbol of stability during tough times. These are the stories that show gold isn't just a metal; it's like a protector of family stories and values. We will deep dive into the details about gold's value later in this book.

## Different Forms of Gold Investments: Your Tales, My Tales, & the Tales of Countless Generations

Gold is a bit like a chameleon in the investment world—it can take on many forms. In my journey in the jewelry business, I've seen gold in all kinds of expressions. From crafting intricate jewelry pieces that narrate tales of love to exploring the weightiness of bullion and the modern coolness of ETFs, each form has a unique story to tell, and each has its place in the journey of wealth preservation.

To summarize, Chapter 3 unfolds the pages of personal and historical stories, enriching our understanding of gold as an investment. It's not just about its market value; it's about the stories

it carries, the stability it offers, and the diverse forms it can take in our lives. I'll be your guide in the upcoming chapters to share the fascinating journey of these different types of gold expressions. Let's remember that gold isn't just an investment; it's a custodian of tales — **your tales, my tales, and the tales of countless** generations.

> Sona, aapki zindagi ke safar mein sirf ek nivesh nahi, saathi ki tarah hai!
>
> **- Manish -**

O    O    O    O

# 4

# Concept Decoded: Hum 2 - Hamare 3

### *Our Journey, Our Balance: Hum 2 - Hamare 2*

"Hum 2, Hamare 2" (Two of us, Two of our family) is like a well-balanced life—two tires for the vehicle and two family members contributing to the journey of life. As we explore why gold becomes not just an investment but the much-needed "3rd child," let's draw a parallel to a common sight on our roads—an extra tire tucked away in the trunk of our cars, commonly called a stepney. Just as a car requires an extra stepney for unforeseen bumps in the road, our financial journey benefits from an additional element—a third child, symbolized by gold."

## *Why We Need a 3rd Child -*
## *The Stepney Theory*

Imagine a long drive, the road stretches ahead, full of promising adventure, but with unexpected challenges waiting to happen. It is at this juncture that the extra stepney becomes crucial. In the reality of life, gold assumes a similar role—a reliable cushion, an extra layer of security for the unexpected twists and turns that life may throw our way.

A stepney tire is always seen as a backup plan, and its importance can be felt during the emergency. Gold, much like a stepney tire, fulfills emergency needs and provides the luxury of security as well. It stands ready, quietly tucked away, yet its presence is felt in times of need. Let's decode the concept of the "3rd child" — an idea transforming gold from an asset to an essential family member, safeguarding our financial journey.

Why do we need a third child, and why equate it to gold? The reason is simple: both gold and a stepney tire offer crucial support. The stepney is a backup, a support system ensuring that the journey continues seamlessly even when faced with unexpected challenges. Gold, likewise, is a tangible asset that preserves wealth, providing stability in times of economic uncertainties.

## *Investing in Your 3rd Child:*
## *Giving Your Future 3x Security*

Just as I invest in my children's education to ensure their growth and well-being, I envision gold as a parallel investment—my 3rd child. Depositing fees of each child and buying equal amounts of Gold has been my main winning strategy ever. This concept goes beyond finances; it's about nurturing and securing your future. As we set aside resources for our children's education to empower them, similarly, investing in gold is a proactive step towards empowering our financial well-being. Imagine your life as a journey of these milestones:

| Stages of Life | 1st child | 2nd child | Investing into your 3rd child - Gold | My Commitment to myself |
|---|---|---|---|---|
| Your Marriage | - | - | You have already received a lot of gold in your marriage. | • Yes, true for me |
| Your Family Starts | First Baby is born | 2nd Baby is born | Buy some gold as a celebration of the birth of your 1st child & then 2nd Child. | • Yes, I will do it. |
| School Admission | School Fee - 1st Child | School Fee - 2nd Child | Buy some gold = the school fee of each child every month/quarter. | • Yes, I should do it, seems systematic & practical. |

| College admission | College fee - 1st Child | College fee - 2nd Child | Buy some gold = the college fee of each child every month/ quarter | • Yes, I should do it, seems systematic & practical. |
|---|---|---|---|---|
| Marriage | 1st son/ daughter getting Married | 2nd son/ daughter getting Married | Again, buying gold & gifting it to your daughter, son, daughter-in-law, or son-in-law | • Yes, true for me. |
| Birthdays & Anniversaries in the family | Every Year | Every Year | Buy some gold on each moment of happiness & celebration | • Yes, I will do it. |
| Yearly occasions where gold buying is considered auspicious | - | - | Gift Gold/ Gold Jewellery to each family member on these occasions. Like,<br>• Akshaya Tritiya<br>• Dhanteras<br>• Diwali | • Yes, I will do it. or I have been doing it. |

## The Balancing Act

Life is like a dance, and balance is crucial. The car moves smoothly with the balanced distribution of weight across its tires. Similarly, our financial portfolio gains resilience through the stability offered by gold. The third child, in the form of gold, balances the financial equation, ensuring that our wealth remains steady even when faced with unforeseen bumps.

As we conclude this chapter, envision the journey of life as a road trip—full of adventures, unexpected detours, and moments of joy. The extra stepney, much like gold, is not just a spare part; it's a companion, a guardian ensuring our journey goes smoothly.

In the chapters that follow, we will talk about the practical aspects of incorporating gold as your 3rd child in your financial strategy. From historical significance to the modern investment landscape, join me as we explore the tangible and emotional aspects of welcoming gold into your family.

# 5

# My Story - 'Shaadi se Saalgirah Tak'

As we navigate the world of gold investments, let's turn our attention to the narratives of others—real people with real experiences. Through anecdotes, personal stories, and timeless lessons, this chapter brings your focus on the seemingly complex world of gold prices, making it relatable and accessible. Much like the memories associated with significant life events, gold prices have their own story. Join me on a journey through time travel as I unfold my experiences with gold prices. Together, we'll explore the highs, the lows, and the turning points that shaped my understanding of gold's dynamic nature.

## And this Question Made me Speechless for a Minute

In the tapestry of my life, there's a moment when the importance of gold investments became crystal clear, intertwined with the memories of my wedding day. It was a day when **My Wife - Suchi,** the voice of my strength, the backbone of my success - asked me a simple yet transformative question: "Apni shaadi mein Gold ka kya bhaav tha, Manish?" And, I was speechless for a minute…

Her inquiry sparked a journey into the history of gold rates, and what I found was amazing. I remember telling her, **"It was exactly 13,800 in February 2010, and today it's around 70,000, my love!"** In that moment, as the numbers echoed in the air, the impact of gold's appreciation over the years became visible. The figures revealed that in the span of 15 years, gold had appreciated almost fivefold.

As I dived deeper into the gold rate history chart immediately (shown here on the next page), a breathtaking realization awaited me. The chart not only highlighted the journey of gold but also unveiled a **fundamental truth — gold appreciates approximately ten times in every 20-year span.** This simple fact surprised me and made me see how important gold is for our financial future.

This incident became more than a mere exchange of numbers; it became a manifestation. The numbers weren't just on a chart; they were woven into the fabric of our life's journey. The realization that gold had become not just an investment but a steadfast companion in our financial growth was transformative. It served as the catalyst, propelling me into a deeper understanding of gold's role in securing our financial future.

## The Charted Journey of Gold:

## Last 75 years

| Year | Rate | % age increase | Year | Rate | % age increase | Year | Rate | % age increase |
|---|---|---|---|---|---|---|---|---|
| 1950 | 99 | - | 1980 | 1300 | 46% | 2003 | 5700 | 14% |
| 1955 | 79 | -20% | 1981 | 1800 | 38% | 2004 | 5800 | 2% |
| 1958 | 95 | 20% | 1982 | 1600 | -11% | 2005 | 7000 | 21% |
| 1960 | 111 | 17% | 1983 | 1800 | 13% | 2006 | 9000 | 29% |
| 1961 | 119 | 7% | 1984 | 1900 | 6% | 2007 | 10800 | 20% |
| 1962 | 119 | 0% | 1985 | 2000 | 5% | 2008 | 12500 | 16% |
| 1963 | 97 | -18% | 1986 | 2100 | 5% | 2009 | 14500 | 16% |
| 1964 | 63 | -35% | 1987 | 2500 | 19% | 2010 | 18000 | 24% |
| 1965 | 71 | 13% | 1988 | 3000 | 20% | 2011 | 25000 | 39% |
| 1966 | 83 | 17% | 1989 | 3100 | 3% | 2012 | 32000 | 28% |
| 1967 | 102 | 23% | 1990 | 3200 | 3% | 2013 | 29600 | -8% |
| 1968 | 162 | 59% | 1991 | 3400 | 6% | 2014 | 28006 | -5% |
| 1969 | 176 | 9% | 1992 | 4300 | 26% | 2015 | 26343 | -6% |
| 1970 | 184 | 5% | 1993 | 4100 | -5% | 2016 | 28623 | 9% |
| 1971 | 193 | 5% | 1994 | 4500 | 10% | 2017 | 29667 | 4% |
| 1972 | 202 | 5% | 1996 | 5100 | 13% | 2018 | 31438 | 6% |
| 1973 | 243 | 20% | 1997 | 4700 | -8% | 2019 | 35220 | 12% |
| 1974 | 369 | 52% | 1998 | 4000 | -15% | 2020 | 48651 | 38% |
| 1975 | 520 | 41% | 1999 | 4200 | 5% | 2021 | 48720 | 0.14% |
| 1976 | 545 | 5% | 2000 | 4400 | 5% | 2022 | 52670 | 8% |
| 1978 | 685 | 26% | 2001 | 4300 | -2% | 2023 | 65200 | 24% |
| 1979 | 890 | 30% | 2002 | 5000 | 16% | 2024 | 72500 | 11% |

देखें...किसकी शादी में सोने का क्या भाव था।
आपको तो कुछ आइडिया भी नहीं होगा।

# 6

# Ek aur Kahani - "Papa ne Kyun Nahi Kharida?"

The heartbeat of this chapter lies in real-life case studies of families who have successfully passed on their legacy through generations, with gold as a central asset. These stories are not just about numbers; they're about the human element, the emotions, and the deliberate choices made by families to protect and grow their wealth.

## Case study 1: 'Kaash...'

As a typical social being, my fuel for growth often comes from the stories shared by friends and family. It was during one such conversation that an interesting incident unfolded, pulling my attention towards gold investment.

**My Brother-In-Law Varun,** questioned with curiosity, remembering the days when gold was more affordable in our father's time - **"Papa ke time pe Gold kitna sasta tha, kaash papa ne us time itne kam rate mein thoda Gold le liya hota, to aaj ye badhte hue rates ki tension nahi hoti,"** he sighed. With a knowing smile, I responded, "No worries, the past has been a great teacher, let's shape our future, let's buy now. So at least, your child would not echo the regret of you not buying the Gold at the right time." And just like that, another chapter unfolded in our family's gold legacy and a chapter of this book.

## *Case study 2: The Gupta Family Chronicles - Gold's Enduring Legacy*

Enter the Gupta family, where gold isn't just an investment; it's a language of love spoken across generations. One of my father's childhood friend, Dr. Subhash Gupta, the family head, vividly recalls the conversations during key life moments. **"I remember purchasing gold jewelry when my daughter got married; it was more than** a financial decision—it was a promise of enduring love and security for her future while we were gifting that jewelry to her at the wedding." The Guptas' story unfolds like a personal diary, with each gold piece carrying the whispers of familial bonds.

## *Case study 3: The Kapoor Family's Intimate Gold Planning*

Now, meet the Kapoors, a family whose intimate conversations about gold echo through the years. "We wanted both of our children to understand the value of continuity. Along with depositing their school fees, we always bought an equal amount of raw Gold and invested in Gold exactly like we invested in our children's education," Mrs. Sumita Kapoor reflected. The couple's evenings were filled with discussions about the significance of gold—how it's not just a metal but a bridge connecting their past, present, and future. The Kapoors' case study reveals a journey fueled not just by financial acumen coupled with continuity but by the warmth of shared dreams and aspirations.

## *Case study 4: The Sharma Family - Gold as the Silent Witness*

In the Sharma family, gold is not just an investment; it's a silent witness to the passage of time. Mrs. Sharma recounts, **"Our family has seen it all—from my mother's wedding to my daughter's wedding day, each Gold piece carries the emotions of laughter, tears, and countless celebrations."** As time passes, the Sharmas consider gold not only as a wealth preserver but as a symbol of shared memories and a testament to the enduring strength of their familial bonds.

## *Case study 5: The Singh Family - Birth to Marriage, Gold as a Guardian*

For the Singh family, gold serves as a guardian from the moment of birth to the sacred vows of marriage. Mr. Kanwardeep Singh fondly shares, **"We started a tradition of gifting gold to our children on their birthdays. It's not just an investment; it's a tradition beyond cake cutting that symbolizes the promise of a secure and prosperous future."** The Singhs' narrative underscores the multi-generational role that gold plays in nurturing family ties.

## *More than Just Insights*

Delving into these intimate case studies, let's gain more than insights into strategic planning; let's witness the heartbeat of familial connections. Each case study becomes a meaningful reminder that wealth transfer isn't just about numbers; it's about the long-lasting legacy of love and foresight.

As we conclude these last 2 chapters, the resonance of "Shaadi se Salgirah tak & Birthday se Anniversary tak" echoes, signifying not just the **passing of wealth but the passing of heart-to-heart conversations, values, and the essence of a family's story.**

# 7

# Setting up the Right Future for this 3rd Child - "Kaun Sa Gold Mere Liye Sahi Hai?"

### *Gold for Every Pocket - Har Kismat Mein Sona Hai*

Just as parenting involves making thoughtful choices for a child's school, college, and career, nurturing your "3rd child" — Gold — also requires care & strategic decision-making.

This chapter shares stories of regular people like us who have found ways to include gold in their lives, no matter their budget. Through these stories, we discover the multiple ways gold can be a part of our financial journey. We'll explore the art of buying and selling gold, providing each one of us with valuable tips and strategies. As we talk about keeping your gold safe, we'll compare it to the important job of raising a child and how it shapes their future.

One such story comes from Dhan Bahadur, a diligent Nepali worker of my shop in Kucha Mahajani, the bustling market of Chandni Chowk. He shared his gold story during a casual conversation,

"Sona toh hum sabke liye hota hai. Main har mahine thoda sa sona baali (Earring) ya angoothi (Ring) ki form mein kharid leta hoon, ek tarah se savings bhi ho jati hai and pehan bhi leta hu. Aajkal toh bahut achha saving scheme bhi chal raha hai." (Gold is for everyone. I save a little gold every month in the form of jewelry for my family; it's a form of savings. Nowadays, there are better savings schemes available.)

Harpreet, a young banking professional, whom I met on a train journey to Vaishno Devi. He shared how he started his gold journey, "Mujhe pehle lagta tha ki sona sirf ameer logon ke liye hota hai, par jab maine ek chhota sa sone ka sikka kharida, tabse main samajh gaya ki ye har kisi ke liye accessible hai." (I used to think gold was only for wealthy people, but when I bought a small gold coin, I realized that gold is accessible for everyone.)

## *Types of Gold: Jewellery, Bullion, Gold Coins or ETFs*

Now, imagine walking into a lively marketplace filled with various options. Gold, too, offers a range of choices — from the ornate beauty of jewelry to the simple purity of bullion, the elegance of Gold Coins, and the modern convenience of ETFs. This section guides you through these choices, explaining their features, benefits, and considerations associated with each. It helps you make informed decisions based on your financial goals and preferences.

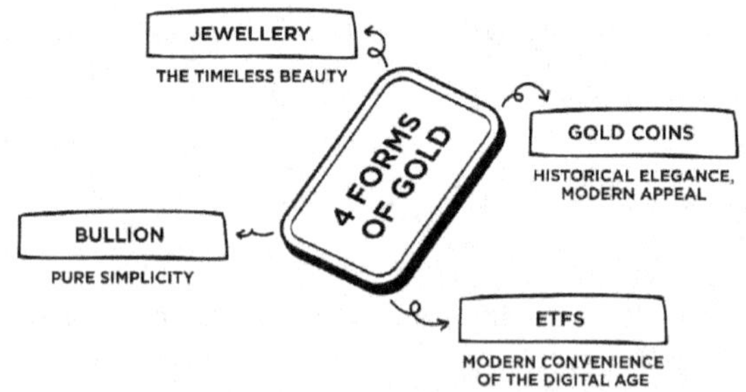

## 1. Jewelry: The Timeless Beauty

Let's start with the traditional beauty of jewelry, made of the precious metal, Gold. With its fancy designs and skilled craftsmanship, jewelry is not just about gold; it's a canvas of traditions and emotions. Beyond being an investment, it carries emotional value and cultural significance. In this world of gold & diamond jewelry, we'll explore the artistry, cultural aspects, and the emotional connection that makes it a unique form of investment & luxury.

## 2. Bullion: Pure Simplicity

Bullion, in its purest form, represents simplicity and substance. This section sheds light on the straightforward nature of gold bullion, discussing its purity, weight, and the role it plays as a tangible asset. You will gain insights into why bullion is considered a timeless and foundational form of gold investment. It's a direct ownership of gold, free from the embellishments of design. Holding bullion is like holding the essence of this precious metal. When you choose bullion, you opt for a straightforward and tangible investment, making you a curator of intrinsic value.

## 3. Gold Coins: Historical Elegance, Modern Appeal

Gold coins bring together the charm of history and the practicality of modern investment. These coins carry not only the weight of gold but also adds an extra layer of convenience to gift to your loved ones on different occasions. When you choose gold coins, you're not just investing; you're getting a piece of history with a touch of elegance. Gold coins; are elegant and easy to carry, a beautiful and smart investment style. The charm of gold coins, their historical significance, collector's value and practical usage, makes it very important for all of us to incorporate a few gold coins into our diversified gold portfolio.

## 4. ETFs: Modern Convenience of the Digital Age

Exchange-Traded Funds (ETFs) bring gold investment into the digital age. They offer a convenient way to gain exposure to the gold market without the need for physical possession. When you choose gold ETFs, you're not just investing; you're embracing the digital evolution of wealth management. The world of gold ETFs has its own structure, benefits, and considerations. One must explore the world of ETFs, understand how they fit into the dynamics of your financial strategy with cost-effectiveness and liquidity.

Think of exploring these different types of gold like choosing the best school for your child. Each form has its unique qualities, and your decision should align with your long-term financial goals and personal preferences. The process of selecting the right form of gold mirrors the careful consideration and planning involved in securing a bright future for your 3rd child.

In the next parts, we'll go deeper into buying, selling, storing, and securing your chosen form of gold. This guide will help you take care of your '3rd child' and make sure your finances grow well.

# 8

# "A mere Gold, ab tu hi bata - Kab Kharidu, Kitna Kharidu aur Kaise Kharidu"

*Buying and Selling Gold: Tips and Strategies*

Buying and selling gold is a bit like managing life's ups and downs. In this section, we delve into the art of navigating these transactions. From understanding market dynamics to timing purchases and sales, you will gain practical tips and strategies. We'll use real-life stories to show you what to do—and what not to do—so you can feel more confident while making decisions about gold.

No matter what type of gold you're dealing with, knowing when to buy and when to sell is very important. Here are some easy tips: Keep an eye on things like how the economy is doing, important events around the world, and how gold prices have changed over time. And here's a smart strategy: try to stay disciplined, buy gold in different ways over time, and think about what you want to achieve in the short and long term.

## Strategic Timing: "The 30-30 ml Theory" (Tho-di-Thodi Piya Karo...)

A few years back when I was in BNI, I introduced a Strategy called the "30-30 ml, oh sorry, 30-30 gm theory," which draws a parallel between drinking habits at a party and investment consistency. Much like staying alert and active till 4 a.m. in the party, you must drink slowly and consistently in the ratio of 30-30 ml (not the Patiala one's in a single shot). Investing steadily in the ratio of 30-30 grams every month ensures a consistent approach in the race of investment versus expenses. It's a practical and relatable way to avoid making rushed investment decisions.

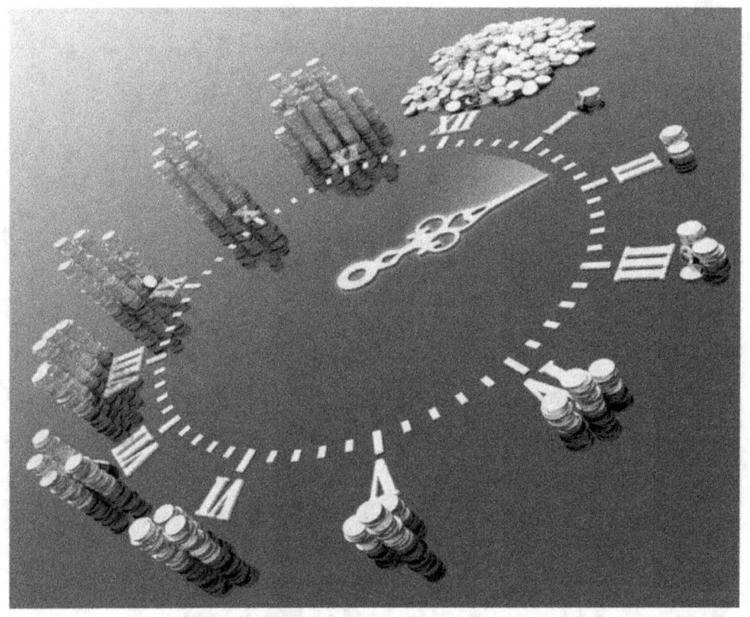

## Eliminating the Risk of Gold Rate Fluctuations

One common question I face almost every day from friends, customers, and relatives is: **"What is the gold rate today, and is it the right time to invest? Will it increase or decrease further? Please suggest, as you have been in the jewelry business for so many years!"** Addressing this uncertainty, I used to humorously suggest, "Let me check with Mr. Modi ji & get back to you!" or even suggest asking Mr. Modi ji directly for this typical advice. However, after deeper exploration and research, I discovered a practical solution—consistent investment in smaller quantities is the key to this uncertainty of gold rate fluctuations.

The 30-30 gm theory offers a systematic approach that broadly averages out the daily fluctuations in gold rates, providing a steady and informed investment journey.

**- Manish -**

Whether you are a seasoned investor or a novice, staying informed is a continuous process. Tips include regular market research, exploring reputable sources, and attending industry events. Seeking professional advice, especially from financial advisors and experts in the field of Gold & Jewellery, forms a strategic approach to navigating the dynamic landscape of buying and selling gold.

## Storing and Securing Your Gold Investments

Much like a child's safety is paramount, securing your gold investments is crucial for their long-term well-being. Let's look at the different options for storing gold. **From home safes** to **bank vaults** and the **emerging realm of digital storage,** investors have all the options available. I'll share practical tips on how to keep your gold safe and minimize risks, so your "3rd child" stays safe and secure on its journey.

## Upbringing is the Key -
## "Acchi Nurturing Bahut Important Hai!"

Let's compare raising a child to nurturing your gold investments. Just like a child's future is shaped by positive influences, your gold investments need smart decisions to grow. Much like raising a child, nurturing your gold investments requires patience, wisdom, and a touch of personal connection.

I vividly recall a moment from my early days of investing in gold. It was a time when the markets were unpredictable, and I, much like a new parent, was learning the ropes. My decision to allocate a portion of my investments to gold was comparable to welcoming a new member to the family.

Just as a parent recognizes the unique qualities and potential in their child, I realized the importance of understanding the intrinsic value of gold. It was not merely a financial asset; it was a silent partner in my journey, ready to support me whenever needed.

## Technological Innovations in Gold Market

As we fast-forward to the digital age, technology plays a central player's role in shaping the landscape of gold investments. We must explore innovations such as digital gold and blockchain, offering a glimpse into the future of gold transactions. Real -world examples of technological integration in the gold market will showcase the opportunities that lie ahead for tech savvy investors.

## *Global Trends Shaping Gold Prices*

In this final part of the chapter, we'll take a journey around the world to see what affects gold prices. From geopolitical tensions to economic fluctuations, there are a lot of factors influencing the value of gold on the international stage. Here are some factors which affect Gold prices, as per my understanding:

➢ **Investor Sentiment:**

- **Market sentiment:** Psychological factors such as fear, greed, and risk aversion influence investor behavior and can lead to rapid changes in gold prices.

- **Speculative activity:** Trading activity in futures markets, options contracts, and exchange-traded funds (ETFs) can amplify price movements, especially during times of heightened uncertainty.

› Geopolitical Events:

- **Political instability:** Uncertainty or unrest in key geopolitical regions can lead investors to seek the safety of gold, driving up demand and prices.

- **Diplomatic tensions:** Heightened tensions between countries can increase risk perceptions, prompting investors to allocate more capital to gold as a hedge against potential fallout.

**Armed conflicts:** Wars or military conflicts can disrupt global markets and currencies, causing investors to flock to gold as a reliable store of value.

› Economic Indicators:

- **Inflation rates:** Rising inflation erodes the purchasing power of fiat currencies, making gold an attractive option to preserve wealth.

- **Currency values:** Fluctuations in currency exchange rates impact the relative value of gold for investors holding different currencies.

- **Interest rates:** Changes in interest rates set by central banks influence borrowing costs, inflation expectations, and investment decisions, all of which can affect gold prices.

› Central Bank Policies:

- **Monetary policy decisions:** Actions taken by central banks, such as adjusting interest rates or implementing quantitative easing measures, can impact currency valuations and investor sentiment towards gold.

- **Gold reserves:** Central banks' buying or selling of gold reserves can directly affect supply and demand dynamics in the gold market.

➤ Geopolitical Developments:

- **Trade disputes:** Tariffs and trade tensions between major economies can disrupt global trade flows and investor confidence, leading to fluctuations in gold prices.

- **Geopolitical unrest:** Events like coups, civil unrest, or regime changes in key gold-producing or consuming countries can influence supply chains and market sentiment.

- **International relations:** Diplomatic shifts, alliances, or conflicts between nations can create uncertainty and drive investors towards safe-haven assets like gold.

Understanding the dynamics of these trends positions you to make informed decisions, guiding you through the market's twists and turns as you pursue your financial goals. In times of high inflation, gold often sees a surge as investors seek a safe haven to safeguard their purchasing power and hedge against the weakening buying power of national currencies like the dollar. Similarly, when geopolitical tensions are high, the price of gold tends to rise as investors seek a hedge against uncertainty. If geopolitical tension or economic uncertainty exists, gold is used to ride out macroeconomic volatility. Still, these correlations don't always hold true; sometimes, gold prices don't go up even when inflation or uncertainty is high.

The price of gold is influenced by its supply and demand dynamics, much like any other commodity. Gold serves various purposes beyond being a store of value, including its use in jewelry and industrial applications like electronics and medical devices, contributing significantly to its demand. The progression of these industries directly impacts the demand for gold.

Additionally, the limited supply of gold, affected by factors such as mining production, exploration efforts, and government policies, also plays a crucial role in determining its price. The marginal cost of producing new gold is another significant factor, as the price tends to increase when deposits become more complex or scarce to access. Conversely, advancements in mining and extraction technologies that enhance efficiency and cost-effectiveness can lead to a reduction in gold prices.

This book is a comprehensive guide to help you navigate the world of gold investments, treating your gold holdings as your "3rd child". Through understanding different forms, transactions, and security measures, you'll gain the confidence to manage your gold with care. Imagine yourself as a nurturing parent, making informed decisions to shape your gold's future. Whether buying or selling, the tips and strategies provided serve as your trusted compass.

# 9

# Is this 3rd Child worth Trusting in the Long Run? - "Zaroorat padne par kaam aayega Na?"

Trust is the cornerstone of any long lasting relationship. When it comes to investments, building trust with your "3rd child" — gold — is most important. In this chapter, we embark on a journey to explore the credibility of gold as a long-term companion.

## Comparing Gold with other Assets

In the busy marketplace of investments, each asset tells a unique tale, offering its distinct set of promises and challenges. Imagine this financial bazaar, and let's explore why gold deserves a prominent role in your investment portfolio.

➢ Think of the stock market like a rollercoaster ride, full of ups and downs.

➢ Bonds, on the other hand, are like a steady ship in calm waters, providing stability.

- ➢ Real estate brings something tangible to the table, adding depth to the story.
- ➢ And then there's **Gold — a unique player that offers stability, growth, and diversification all rolled into one.**

Picture a family gathering where different investment options are like characters at the dinner table. Stocks are the talkative relatives, always chatting away, bonds bring a sense of calm, and real estate stands strong like the sturdy pillar of the family home. In the midst of it all, gold sits quietly, its timeless charm catching the eye of the observant family member. As the discussion unfolds, it becomes clear that gold isn't an outsider but an essential member of the family.

## *Gold & Trust go Hand in Hand*

Through this chapter, we set out to answer a crucial question: Is gold worth trusting in the long run? By comparing gold with other assets, exploring its digital evolution, and assessing its contribution to sustainable investing, you gain a comprehensive view of gold's long lasting relevance in life. **Trust becomes the bridge that connects you with the timeless value of gold,** making it not just an investment, but a reliable and trustworthy ally in the journey of financial well-being.

Let me make it more clear by another personal analogy. **Gold functions similar to a blood bank.** It sits there as idle as life flows normally, but its importance becomes paramount in times of emergency. Just like blood is crucial for life, gold becomes an indispensable asset when financial emergencies arise. This perspective transforms gold from just another asset to a lifeline, a reliable companion that holds its value even in turbulent times.

# 10

## Better Bonding for Better Relations - "Rishtey Banane Se Badhane Tak!"

*Cultural and Emotional Attachments to Gold*

Gold isn't just about money; it carries a lot of feelings too. In this chapter, we delve into the deep connections individuals and families have with gold. It's not just shiny metal; it's part of our culture, our celebrations, and our family stories.

We'll explore how gold is tied to big events like weddings and festivals, and how families pass down gold jewelry through generations. With stories and examples, you have already seen how gold isn't just an investment—it's like a member of the family.

Let me share a personal story from my own family to show you what I mean. **We have this special Gold 'Tagdi' that has been passed down through generations.** It's not just a piece of jewelry; it's a living testament to the cultural and emotional significance attached to gold. This Tagdi, worn by my grandmother on her wedding day & then by my mother and now by my wife, holds stories of love, resilience, and familial bonds. Wearing such articles not just adds to your beauty but brings a feeling of attachment, warmth & emotions. Stories like these show how gold is more than just a metal; it's part of our history and our family legacy.

## Overcoming Common Misconceptions

Sometimes, misunderstandings can cloud our thinking and hold us back from seeing things clearly. I've had my own eye-opening experiences. When I first started investing in gold, I thought it was just a boring, unchanging asset. But the more I learned, the more I realized how gold can actually move and change with the times, fitting right into modern investment strategies. Getting past these misconceptions will help you see through the fog of myths, giving you the confidence to make smart choices.

## Balancing Sentiment with Financial Goals

**Balancing sentiment with financial goals is not a science but an art,** one that requires a learner's approach. When my family decided to liquidate some gold assets to fund an important life event, the decision wasn't purely financial; it was a harmonious blend of sentiment and strategy. Such real-life stories navigating this balance will inspire you to approach your gold investments with both heart and mind. This section isn't just a guide; it acts as a companion in the reader's own journey of finding equilibrium between sentiment and financial prudence.

As we finish up this chapter, we've talked about how gold isn't just about money—it's also about culture, emotions, and getting rid of misunderstandings. Gold isn't just something you buy and sell; it's a link between different generations, cultures, and feelings. **Gold is not just an investment it's an integral part of our shared human experience.**

# 11

# Navigating Market Volatility - "Thought to Action - sahi soch se sahi samay par sahi step tak!"

In the dynamic landscape of investments, market volatility is a constant companion. This chapter is here to help you steer through these uncertain waters, providing tips for investing when things get stormy. From learning valuable lessons from historical gold market movements to building psychological resilience in gold investing, you will gain insights into making informed decisions amidst market fluctuations.

## *Strategies for Investing in Turbulent Times*

Market turbulence can be unsettling, but it also presents opportunities for strategic investors to buy at lower prices. We should always be ready with the strategies for navigating turbulent markets. From adopting a long-term perspective to diversifying portfolios, we should make sound investment decisions even when faced with uncertainty. In real-life, strategic thinking can turn market challenges into opportunities.

## *Learning from Historical Gold Market Movements*

History serves as a valuable teacher in the world of investments. Chapter 5 of this book clearly illustrates - gold rate history, trends of the industry & past 60 years movements. By understanding historical patterns explained into various chapters of this book, readers can better anticipate and respond to market dynamics.

## *Emotions vs Gold Investment*

Investment decisions can be significantly influenced by emotions, particularly when faced with market volatility. The ability to set realistic expectations and maintain discipline, especially during volatile periods, became a key factor in my success. We should carefully look into the insights fostering a mindset that withstands the emotional highs and lows of investing. Handling market changes means not just thinking strategically but also being able to make quick decisions. Learning from past moves, sticking to proven strategies, and staying mentally strong are all key to navigating the twists and turns of the investment world.

# 12

# Celebrating Birth of 3rd Baby - "Kya Hum Tayyar Hain?"

As we near the end of our journey together, it's time to celebrate the birth of your "3rd child" - Gold - and empower you with the knowledge and confidence to make smart Gold investments.

## *Gold as a Booster for Faster Wealth Growth*

From understanding gold as your "third child" to recognizing its historical significance, navigating economic changes, and embracing gold as a means to leave a lasting legacy, we've delved into various aspects of gold investments. Throughout this journey, we've seen how adding gold to your financial portfolio can be like adding rocket fuel to your savings, propelling them to new heights.

**But this book isn't just about theoretical concepts; it's about real people making real decisions that impact their financial futures.** Through the stories, tips and tricks shared throughout this book , you've seen how individuals have taken charge of their financial destinies by incorporating gold into their investment strategies.

These stories offer relatable examples of how ordinary people have used gold to overcome financial challenges, secure their futures, and achieve their dreams.

## Life Does Give Choices Only If You Take Them!

Absolutely, life is all about the choices we make, and that holds true for our financial decisions as well. By highlighting the importance of investment strategies, I encourage you to take a proactive approach in aligning your financial choices with your values, aspirations, and long-term goals.

Real-life stories of individuals who took charge of their financial destinies through gold investments add a personal touch to this book, offering relatable examples of how ordinary people have leveraged gold to navigate financial challenges, secure their futures, and achieve their dreams.

## Having Gold as Your 3rd Child
## Is Like a Gift You Can Give Yourself

We wrap up our journey by celebrating the special bond you can build with gold. The expression of gold as a gift—one that brings joy, security, and a sense of accomplishment—is explored. You are invited to view gold not just as an investment but as a child or a companion into the family that enhances their financial well-being and contributes to the legacy they leave for future generations.

Now, it's time to celebrate the birth of this new child, gold, into your financial family. Just as parents eagerly anticipate the arrival of a new baby, you can anticipate the growth and prosperity that gold will bring into your life. Embrace this new addition to your portfolio with enthusiasm and confidence, knowing that it will play a vital role in your financial well-being for years to come.

> Like a newborn, gold represents a fresh start,
> a new chapter in your financial journey.
> It's a symbol of hope, potential, and the
> promise of a brighter future.
>
> **- Manish -**

# MASTER YOUR INVESTMENT HABITS

## *Summary of the book*

# 7 Rock-Solid Reasons Why You Should Adopt Gold as Your 3rd child?

Alright, so after reading this book, we can definitely summarize a few points and dive into why putting your money into gold is one of the smartest moves you can make. Let's break it down into seven juicy reasons, spiced up with some real-life tales:

➤ **Gold's Timeless Charm:** Picture this - gold has been wowing people since, well, forever! It's like that friend who's always there, dependable and shiny. Back in the day, your great-great-great-grandparents were probably singing its praises, and guess what? It's still rocking the show today. *That's the kind of stability you want in your investment portfolio. Don't you?*

➤ **A Solid, Tangible Asset:** Ever held a gold coin in your hand? It's like holding a piece of history and a chunk of your future all at once. *Unlike those digital Rupees that can vanish in a blink, gold is as real as it gets.* Having some gold tucked away is like having a superhero in your financial arsenal, ready to rescue you when things get rough in the economy.

➤ **Diversification, Baby!:** Imagine putting all your eggs in one basket - not a smart move, right? Well, gold is your ticket to diversifying like a pro. *When the stock market throws a*

——∘○○-○○∘——

*tantrum or the real estate market goes haywire, gold's got your back. It's like having a backup plan for your backup plan.*

➢ **Beating the Inflation Blues:** Let's talk real talk - money loses its mojo over time. What buys you a pizza today might barely cover a slice in a few years. But gold? It's like that cool kid who never goes out of style. *When inflation comes knocking, gold stands tall, holding onto its value like a champ.*

➢ **Family Heirloom Vibes:** Remember that shiny necklace your grandma passed down to your mom, who's now eyeing it for you? *That's the power of gold - it's not just an investment; it's a piece of your family's story. Investing in gold isn't just about the numbers; it's about creating a legacy that'll make your grandkids proud.*

➢ **Gold Goes Global:** Here's the deal - gold speaks a universal language. Whether you're chilling in New York or sipping chai in Mumbai, *Gold is just Gold*. Its value is recognized worldwide, making it the ultimate global asset in your investment portfolio. *Plus, it's super liquid, so you can cash in whenever, wherever.*

➢ **Securing Your Financial Future:** Let's cut it short - investing in gold is like building a fortress around your finances. Whether you're dreaming of retirement on a beach or sending your kids to international schools, Gold is there to support you. *It's the safety net you didn't know you needed until you did.*

So, finally you have it - *Seven rock-solid reasons to jump on the Gold train but definitely with the seatbelts on,* because it's not just about making money; it's about securing your future, honoring your past, and riding the waves of financial freedom

So, are you ready, or are you still waiting for my next book?

## Roadmap - "Aage ka Raasta"

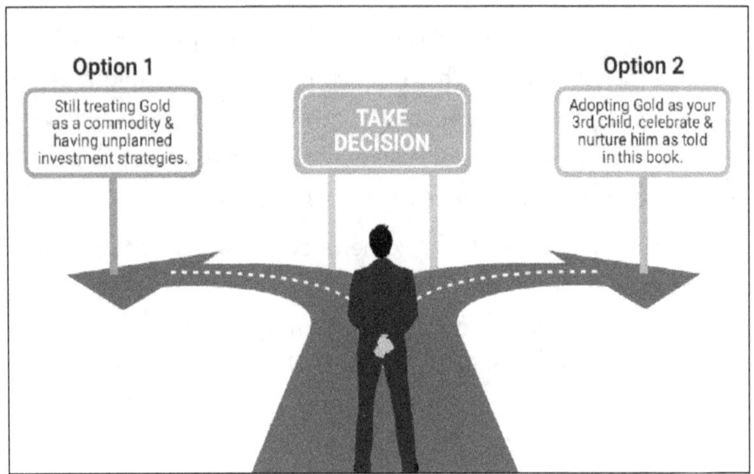


## *Tired of Saving Slow?*

## *Unlock 20x Faster Growth with Gold!*

➢ Struggling to save for your dreams?

➢ What if you could save 20x faster?

➢ Discover the transformative power of gold as your "3rd child" to supercharge your savings!

➢ Understand how to unlock the Gold Secret!

## Join me for a FREE Consultation Every Saturday/Sunday (10 am - 1 pm):

➢ Deep dive into personalized investment strategies.

➢ Learn how gold can accelerate your savings journey.

➢ Book your spot now!

Click here to WhatsApp me:

*https://we.me/919999486668*

*OR Scan the QR Code to schedule your FREE personal consultation with me.*

*This is purely based on my commitment to support you in your investment success!* Invest in gold today and secure a brighter tomorrow for yourself and your loved ones. This concludes our journey through "Gold as Your 3rd Child." *May your investments shine bright, and may the legacy of gold continue to enrich your life for generations to come.*

*P.S.* Stay tuned for my upcoming book - the ultimate roadmap to save 20x faster!